Foucault's
Snails

Foucault's Snails

DIANA MEDLICOTT

THE CHOIR PRESS

First published in the United Kingdom in 2020 by
The Choir Press

ISBN 978-1-78963-148-7

For my children and grandchildren,
from whom I have learnt so much

Contents

⟡

Introduction

Making shopping lists or lists of tasks, composing letters, writing essays, diaries, poems or books – it seems to me that there is nothing so intoxicating or satisfying as laying words down on paper or screen. There they sit, in all their magic, independent and set free. You stare at them but cannot explain how they got there. The process is a wonderful mystery.

The poet R. S. Thomas said that poetry arrives at the intellect by way of the heart. This is a particularly resonant remark for me, because for some years it was part of my job as an academic to write with my intellect, and largely to put a lid on matters of the heart. I loved the business of turning my research into writing, because it fulfilled my desire to analyse the workings of the system, to work for change, and to bear witness for those who had no voice. But it didn't often offer opportunities to show the delight in my heart, and my wonder at the world. Poetry offers this. It's a way of pinning down those intense feelings of heightened awareness that sometimes sweep over one unpredictably, often at quite mundane points in one's life.

In particular it offers the opportunity to try and catch the essence of those feelings one experiences in a new and strange place. I'm a great believer in Place Identity – the idea that places powerfully shape the contours of our minds and behaviours. It was one of my favourite themes when doing research with prisoners, because they all responded so meaningfully to my questions about their significant places. And I've found it a perennial feature of my own life.

I have read poetry all my life. It has always been a true friend – enduring, enlightening, and inspiring. It sometimes feels as if an experience becomes all the more vivid, seen through the prism of a favourite poem. Moments of love, longing, delight, grief and all the panoply of human experience can be distilled in a poem. That's not to say I am satisfied with *my* distillation – often it seems like something is just out of reach, and the longing to set down a poem about that particular experience is limited by my mind's ability to fashion it into something coherent. My poem Slipping is a prime example of this. I know exactly what the feeling is when I wander alone through the woods, but putting it into words … I've been trying to write that poem for ten years, and still it isn't just how I want it.

However, time is passing, and I've come to the conclusion that I would like to see a selection of my poems between book covers, draw a line under thoughts I've been tinkering with for decades and move on to other thoughts. When I wrote academic material, of course I hoped it would bring about change, but I somewhat lost interest in it the minute it was in the public domain. The process was the thing I loved. But with my poems, I know I am going to feel pleasure at seeing them on the page, keeping each other company – friendly snails creeping across the page, from my subjectivity into yours. Hopefully you will recognise some of the thoughts, and occasionally think "Yes! That's sort of how it is for me, too", or "Ooh, no, that's not how it is for me, at all!"

Dreams

In Words, In Games

I never knew you at all, Michel Foucault –
But, for a time, your work went like an arrow to my soul.
You said language was never innocent
And ever after I saw words as monstrous creatures
Some creeping through slime and leeching onto surfaces
With terrible suckers; some pretending, some flattering
All *La-di-da* and *Look At Me*
While behind their veneer they slit your heart
For a slice of cheese or an easy laugh.

Once I dreamt of you: on a long train journey through France
You sat beside me and as we slid through stations
Glimpsing railwaymen in Atlantic blue serge
You made everything clear, speaking rapidly in a monotone.

On waking, words had a new translucence
And I could see that some indeed had purity
Like raindrops on glass or treble notes dropped into silence
Whilst others deceived, assaulted, cajoled, mocked.

Well. Words are snails' trails: sometimes they are the worst of us
And always they show the ways we try to plane our world and
      plumb the rules.

All that enchantment from your work is long ago
And I do own many, many words now that brush my mind
With a loving touch and a sense of repose.

Name-Checking My Heroes, or
Tea at The Chelsea Hotel

Alexandra Kollontai
Won't you sit and drink some chai?
You're my favourite Russian lady
Kinda left and kinda shady.

Leonard Cohen's looking dark
At William Morris defining Art.
Pass the snails and roll a ciggy
Disagreement's not a biggy.

Pablo Neruda, hand on heart
Raises politics to Art.
Nina Simone is one cool chick
She and Pablo really click.

Michel Foucault's over there
Epistemologically mid-air
Gauloise held in elegant fingers
The whiff of Madness somehow lingers.

Harriet Harman, Tony Benn
Socialism will come – but when?
Rufus Wainright, Rosa Parkes
Singing, laughing, making sparks.

Elvis doesn't say a heap
But he smoulders, full of heat.
Charlotte Mew looks all shook up
Sloshing gin in her tea-cup.

Who knew Andy talked so buff
On tennis, poetry and stuff!
Deep in chat with Prince Kropotkin
Knocking back the gut-rot gin.

Henry James is holding court
Perfect clauses streaming forth.
"Seriously" says Johnny Mac
"This grass you're serving packs a whack."

Frederick Chopin's looking ill
Neruda's pushing words uphill
Lorca speaks of glorious Spain
And times that cannot come again.

Conversation sometimes stutters
With every word that Chekhov utters:
Dear Jane Austen's taking notes
As Anton climbs beneath the coats.

History, music, works of art
Clatter clatter goes my heart
Tennis, poetry and life
Favourite people, loving strife.

This is such an awesome blast
Raising heroes from the past!
Such a buzz of brilliant chat
Leonard can I try your hat?

You have all enriched my days
Lit my heart, informed my gaze.
But of course you'll never know it
I'm just an old imposter poet
Bent on penning a Thank You –
Paying homage where it's due.

Navy Blue Days

Days of my girlhood
A lover golden of skin
Navy blue sea the medium
The scent – yellow jasmine.

Into the sea I slid you
Cake mixture off a knife
Now your bones are shells
Your eyes devoid of life.

Words came to haunt me
And shaking I turned away
As you sank, so did the sun
Ending the endless day.

Days of my girlhood,
An episode so strange -
I do not dwell on it much
Except on navy blue days.

Future Present

His grandmother gave him a gift:
It was called A Book
She hid it from the culture reapers
Now he must hide it too.

She showed him words
Black and stoic, they clung
To this rough and creamy surface:
They could not be moved.

Paper became an outlawed word
When the trees all died.
He has seen an image of a tree
He pressed a key and it was gone.

This book – a strange and solid mystery!
Next day, words remained within it
Heroic ants, persistent and stable
He pressed them but they did not vanish.

She says they will be there tomorrow
And tomorrow and tomorrow.
Some made him angry, whilst
Others left him becalmed with peace.

The Golden Carp Yearns for the Moon

(A tribute to the submerged villages all over Spain,
flooded in order to create reservoirs)

Beneath the open window in the dying light
She lies in a bucket of water
A curved comma, her scales
Pearly and pink and glittery gold.
Her fishy eye is fixed upon the sky
And the thin crescent moon.

Once her medium was air: before the waters came
She'd lie beneath her father's olive tree
Laughing of an evening with her boy
A nut- brown maid, a golden soul
Gazing through the latticed branches
She yearned to merge herself with the thin crescent moon.

In old age she lived in a stone house
Grew figs and shelled almonds
Using the gaps in her blackened teeth.
When the waters came, she changed her form
As easily as a dress, and with a gulp
Swam up and up, never looking down.

When the reeds turned brown and slimy
She learned to use them as a gentle comb
To shed the scales that overgrew her gills.
For tens of years, she leapt and soared
Her crescent shapes were legends of the lost
Tales of her neighbours whose forms had ceased to be.

In the morning the golden carp is gone, and the catcher
Runs his thumb around the empty bucket's rim
Catching some loose scales, he holds them to the light.
In the evening, still enchanted, he gazes at the sky
And wonders a little at the pinky golden rim
Around the hard silver of the crescent moon.

August 2009

Slipping

Do you know the other realm
That shadows all we do?
Have you slipped into its mystery
And listened to its force?

Perhaps you've stood in shaded woodlands
Soul stretching to that sudden jolt of joy
Not knowing what the key was, or who turned it
But just aware that there the Keeper rules.

There are no words to make a lasting record
You will not touch the essence though you try
Perhaps you'll hear a sigh like wind through brushwood
And catch a look from each to each, from eye to eye.

This isn't faith or heathen pagan ritual
It isn't your encounter with your god
It's more like ancient re-connection with
The source that time unplugged and quite forgot.

If you don't know this other place or substance
Go deep into the woods and stand quite still
You'll glimpse the Keeper flit between the branches
You'll slip from here and now to ancient realm.

The Keeper animates our sense of being
She calls us back to walk the woods again
The Keeper holds the ones who really matter
Those who yearn and those who suffer pain.

The shadows jump and aid our slipping
The trees throw back the key and let in light
The Keeper never leaves us unregarded
She keeps us all within her kindly sight.

Brother

I dreamt that dream again last night:
A vivid family gathering
Our parents smiling, brown and happy
All our combined children there
Running races, chaotic cousins
We slipped into our old roles
You calm, rational, loud, in charge
Me compliant, fearful, peace-making.
As we ran down a green meadow
Toward a turquoise sea
I asked if you would ever live in England again
And you said, firmly, not.

And that was indeed so:
You returned as ashes in a brown box
Our roles reversed, our threads forever cut
My beloved old adversary: compliant at last.

Places

A Month in Prague

The rowan trees in Biskupcova
Are hoarding clumps of scarlet berries
The chestnuts mimic spiky limes
Trams like tumbrils stutter past
Sledging over cobbles
Their retreating sound ascends the scale
Querulously.

Today in Biskupcova two men heft
An old chest fridge, circa 1955, onto
The roof of a Skoda, once silver.
Under the neurotic glare of two thin dogs
They pack it round with old grey blankets.
Onto it flutter two dried out leaves, almost
Tenderly.

Another day in 1945, Josef Levinsky
Was executed here, and two days later
Alois Pekarek. Today a butterfly
Alights on their plaque: perhaps it hears
The furtive sound of muffled hooves
Some shots at dawn, shame and grief
Unutterable.

Today in Biskupcova two men turn
And walk to where I'm sitting on
Some bricks beside a broken drain.
They fire consonants like needles
Black gap smiles, sandpaper handshakes
Where am I going? My shrugs provoke their
Puzzlement.

But how can I say where I'm going?
I'm here, and here is now in Biskupcova.
The world turns, but this is now my place
Sensing the fit of the rowan tree
The butterfly, the plaque and the broken drain
The click as the tram changes track
And the warmth of strangers
Flowing forward in the warm wind.

Melbourne Fragment

Unfamiliar city, I walk you as an amateur
Your sounds are strange to me, and I record my favourites:
The ding of the tram, and its retreating shuffle
The chittering birdsong and the rising inflexion in the voices
    all around.
Here I leave behind the usual interiors of my mind
Stepping into the spaces in-between
My thoughts slow to match my pace
Across the sandstone cobbles.
And as I stop to sit in Federation Square
Pondering the beauty of the word Yarra
I am suddenly drenched in memories of birdsong long ago
Another Australian city, and those busy days
Of small brown feet in painted sandals
Which can never come again.

January 2013

At the Mutitjara Water-Hole

Far from home, I sit beside the Mutitjara water-hole
In a hot dry wind that passes over me, indifferent.
Lungkata and Lira are not the stories of my people's past
My mind cannot do justice to the wondrous dreamtime
For this place is your quietude, not mine.
And yet, and yet, there are prints in the ochre earth
For the land has gently marked the passage of my feet.
And when I sit to write, the zebra finches stay close
And lift their snub orange beaks to my presence.
The desert oaks, the red rocks, the spiniflex
Are unfamiliar, and yet not other to me: the still air
Throws back to me the sound of my own breath.
I am enfolded by the land
By history, red and still.

Januart 2013

Walking the Loop

We started in the sharp wet days of March, pushing through
    the mud to Haefer's royal palace.
Too busy talking, we missed the silent run of giant sequoias,
    standing indifferent to our passing.
Watched by Dick Turpin's ghost, chimneys loomed, the
    manufactures of then and now,
Tilda rice, raw silk, gunpowder sheds, the green turf barrows
    of London's dirt.

The river, now on our right, bore evidence of flood, of
    industry and man's defences,
Concrete barges, their workdays done, sat mutely in the sullen
    mudflats.
Curlews, redwings, avaricious gulls wheeled mockingly
    overhead,
And so we trudged, from Rainham on to Purfleet, tracing the
    timeline in a concrete arch.

Spurred on by lemon sponge and walnut cake, we skirted the
    beautiful Cray,
Refreshed by its clear cool water, bright red algae and lush
    green reeds.
By now we were into the long warm days of summer, as we
    crossed fairways,
Climbed so very many stiles, and learned to love squeeze
    posts, kissing gates, waymarks.

Deep in Petts Wood, William Willett saved our daylight, as
birch, pine, sweet chestnut
Gave way to sweeping swathes of grassy downland,
Rich with yellow rattle, vetch, cow parsley and the thrumming
noise of bees,
The lavender harvest a sweet-smelling burst of purple plenty,
armfuls of it.

Reaching the western flank, we were besieged by antlered deer,
huge in the flats of Bushy Park;
From there we laboured on beneath the busy flight paths
overhead, disgorging noise and dirt,
Before we came to calmer canals and languid boats, and then
more woodland,
To autumn days, to amber jewelled leaves, irridescent before
our eyes, beneath our feet.

Were we pilgrims? Did we trespass? Talking walkers, what old
and wise green folk saw us pass?
Sometimes it seemed the ancient trees sighed: just out of sight,
the woodfolk wished us well,
Tinkers, gypsies, charcoal burners, only separated from us by
the slipping veil of time.
And weaving our green ribbon round our City, we forged
links, each of us to each, and to the land.

4th March – 5th December 2014
Dedicated to A.M., G.M., M.N., E.Y., and our tireless leader M.F.

Afternoon In Gukurcuk

You are a word warrior: thoughts fly high, concepts glitter.
Aeons, nations, races, ideologies collide in talk
That cuts, divides, segments and sorts
Before opening up new depths into which we fall.

Meanwhile hot mirages shimmer in the shadeless groves
And ancient scenes are glimpsed:
Some wood goddess, tired after hunting, lies down
And soothes her panting hounds beneath an olive tree.

This is not the time to cut the air with talk
Not when this warm peach demands pressing
To your lips, and the dribbled juice asks for
Quick licks and the tidying action of a kiss.
Do you know your eyes grow ever lighter
The longer we lie here?
Such things drop softly into the hot hush of afternoon
Moving the leaden stillness of the air.

When sunset comes, pick up your armour
And I will draw my ancient bow.
Thought can run on quickened hooves once more,
But not words now, dear heart, not words.

Donkey-Shed Days

I had a shed in Andalucia
At the foot of the Alpujarras:
Donkeys lodged in bygone days
Nightly came their ghostly brays.

I had a shed in Andalucia
At the foot of the Alpujarras
Secretive villages, blood-drenched ground
Where History tramped its grim old round.

I took a lover in Andalucia
At the foot of the Alpujarras
How I loved his golden skin
And the muddled heart within.

Picking oranges in Andalucia
Wading rivers on summer nights
Lying under ancient trees
Dreamt and dreaded autumn's breeze.

Simple were my joys back then
In my Andalucian shed
Star-gazing nights, mountains dark
Mine a calm and placid heart.

That little home in Andalucia
That stack of wood, the hungry stove
The stretching heavens, the lemon tree –
All, forever, still with me.

Waves in Kardamyli

Every day we met in the sea
You round and comely in your white hat
We shared one word in common
It held a thousand thoughts.
One day I was late and
Sitting in the square with coffee
I saw you return from your swim.
We shared waves, smiles, mimes
Before the old village, flat cobbles
Swallowed you up. I longed to follow you
Watch you water your jasmine, salt your olives
Bake bread – instead I went to the sea
Breasted the waves and thought about your life.

August 2017

Times

Early Days of Grief

If only I could think of you
stretched peacefully in the clasp of
turf and roses
your hair still bright with its sweep of white
your head turning to follow the swallow's flight
sighing when the waves at sea
billow on stormy nights
your breath joining the cosmic sigh of
energy rippling across the globe.
If only I could dream of you.

1914, Glimpsed from 2014

Your radio voice reaches me from the Great War
You speak of blown-off legs, the stench of pus
The grasping mud, the heartless noise
And all that love forever soaked in pain.
You stroked a dying comrade's hand
And held his wife's picture before his fading eyes
Such fear, such friendships, those craters swallowing lives
The scale, the loss – my mind cannot grasp it.
Some lucky chance of gender and history
Gave me a life that has been rooted
In a life-long tumble of shiny days
Glimpses of the mountains at dawn
The song of blackbirds, streaked skies
But, above all, in birth and births.
Not mud, not death.

Process

These days, these May days
I think of you so much
Reminders seem everywhere, all at once
Bach's Toccata on the radio
Magnolia buds, tight and prissy
Before their eager burst into glory
Horse chestnut candles, laden on the trees
Ready to burst into speech.

What an enigma mothers are: so much life lived before
Babies come and change their hearts for ever.
How can we know our parents before their changed parental
    state?
How can we see the inner growth that ends in chestnut
    blooms?
We can only wonder but not see the journey
Or the You you were to me.

The Spoils of War

We crossed the border at night
A soldier, downy-cheeked, too young to shave
Lolled sleeping on my shoulder
Yugoslavia ended, Greece began.
It was peacetime then
Chickens on the floor in cages
Clucked and fluttered.
My heart in its own cage
Fluttered with pity
For all the boys, the boys
Who join to be brave and good
And only succeed in losing their virtue
Coarsened by conflict
Their minds rubbed raw
By things they saw.
These boys, all spoilt by war.

February 1971

After Torture

What must it be like
to have had those things done to you
by someone who wanted to do such things
and yet was apparently human
what must it be like
to have lost sons
seen daughters despoiled
the beloved, disappeared, all gone
forever decimated
dust bowls for the soul
what must it be like
to have known all that
and still your face shines with hope and truth.

Shearing Time

When I was a child I watched my father
Trimming hedges and edging lawns
I liked the sounds and smells
The clip-clop shears and the pauses in between
The pungent sprucey sappy green.

I never asked what he was thinking
As he snipped and chopped and shaped
Now as I ply my shears and stop to view my work
I think I know. He was dreaming down
The long yesterdays and the shorter tomorrows
I cannot ask him now, my dear old pa
But oh! I wish I could!
For, gathered into the great indifferent folds
He has been sheared by time.

Pieces of the Jigsaw

The ear of the Gruffalo lies listening on the table
Half a pirate's eye scowls by the sink
A dinosaur's claw reaches out
Solitary on the kitchen bench
And all these pieces await your benign restoration
To their own worlds, each contained in a single stacked box.

In your absence I sit in the comfort of your ordered kitchen
All the rooms lie silent, waiting for small bare feet
And the cascade of voices, carolling up and down the stairs
Piles of tenderly smoothed clean clothes
 A scrubbed pine table, a bowl of fruit
Logs stacked in the fireplace, and outside the garden
Holding its breath while the rose petals fall, fall, and drift
Each element part of the chemistry of home.

Sometimes I think my heart will burst
To see the love you put into the raising of
Small important people. Only those who have done it
Day after weary day, can know the zest it needs
And taste the endlessly renewed magic
Each day brings.

September 2014

Delivered by a Standard Form

Here's an 18th birthday boy
This his allotted cell
These his filthy crusty walls
Those his stains of blood and sick
These his wasted boyish limbs
This the heavy heartless door
These his biscuits and packet soup
Delivered by a standard form.

He will not cross the threshhold
Of the daily opened door
He will not go to get his food
And no-one will bring it in.
He says he is a combat soldier
Living wild when war is done
Today I was delivered by a standard form
And when I leave he weeps.

COVID-19

Is this how our extinction begins?
A pestilence that tracks us down?
No celestial impact, no diplodocus
Lost and starving on the crater's rim
Just a creep of morbid stealth
Into our blessèd plots, our care homes.
We locked down: shameful words –
Isolation, distance, shunning –
Became honourable practices.
The earth sighed, worn out with
Our rapacious greed for growth
She took a breather, skies got bluer
Air got cleaner, fish jumped higher.
Then came drought, famines, locusts, lice
Slowly the lessons dawned:
We do not need so much
Whilst many need so much more
Earth needs her snails to trace
More virtuous words of fairness, justice
And trail them through every land
May we reverently green our planet
Its oceans, ice caps, forests, fields
With kindness, kindness, kindness.

May 2020

Like No Other

When that baby came
Her skin was downy like a peach
And all the birds fell silent.
When that baby came
The golden leaves gave up their hold
And fell into the wonder.

When that baby came
The snows followed soon after
And under their weight
The garden paused for breath.
A robin covered the snowy lawn with arrows
And the world sang, gloriously happy.

March 1982

Songs

Smallholding

Ain't got no time for them
Boo hoo songs, them sad guitars
Ain't got the juice to moan
Over what he said, she said
Not when them pigs waitin' to be fed
Go squeeze them oranges and feed the hens
Lock that gate and shake down the jars
Loves dies or it don't
Either way there's bairns to feed
Folks fall in fall out
He said, she said oh what the heck
Get over it you ain't got time
Life be a-passin' and the sun's goin' down.

January 2013

Baker Boy Blues

Ain't no call for you to look at me like that;
Bread needs bakin' and I ain't stoppin' to flirt
You long-legged girlies ain't got no notion
Of work that renders summat outta dirt.

You want some loaves and buns and bagels?
I'm your man and that's the bottom line
But don't go lookin' for some chit-chat baby
Dough's a-risin', and that's what sets my time.

> Oh flour's white or browny speckled
> Them's the only colours ever in my sight
> No chance of blonde, brunette or redhead
> Oh yeah, I got the baker boy blues alright.

Funny how the warm yeast seems to draw them
They linger, giggling round the open door
Dough's a-swellin', and the temperature's risin'
But I can't stop to help it rise some more.

> Oh flour's white or browny speckled
> And it's a-chokin' me real bad
> I ain't got breath for nothin' fancy
> Just like my pa and his ole wheezin' dad.

Oh flour's white or browny speckled
I seem to feel it in my soul at night
The dust is handed down from years before me
Yessir, we got the baker boy blues alright.

August 2004

Her Grandmother's Gown

If only you could see my bright girl
Her hair caught up on the gentlest of necks
The oyster satin of your wedding gown
Falling like water, so easeful and light
Falling like water, so easeful and light.

If only you could hear her molten voice
Holding the room in a state of grace
Faces stopped in stillness
For one song, and then another.

If only you could hold her
She being soft, both cool and warm
All at once, as young girls are
Smelling of the future.

But you, having gone from us
Are as a moth, seen briefly on the edge of lamplight
Brushing lightly the ivory of her neck
And opening the hand-sewn embroidered satin case
In which to put the gown away
Falling like water, so easeful and light
Falling like water, so easeful and light.

2003